ARCANA

Arcana Vol. 3

Created by So-Young Lee

Translation - Youngju Ryu
English Adaptation - Barbara Randall Kesel
Copy Editor - Hope Donovan
Retouch and Lettering - Gloria Wu
Production Artist - Rafael Najarian
Cover Design - Thea Willis

Editor - Bryce P. Coleman
Digital Imaging Manager - Chris Buford
Production Managers - Jennifer Miller and Mutsumi Miyazaki
Managing Editor - Lindsey Johnston
VP of Production - Ron Klamert
Publisher and E.I.C. - Mike Kiley
President and C.O.O. - John Parker
C.E.O. - Stuart Levy

A TOKYOPOP® Manga

TOKYOPOP Inc.
5900 Wilshire Blvd. Suite 2000
Los Angeles, CA 90036

E-mail: info@TOKYOPOP.com
Come visit us online at www.TOKYOPOP.com

ISBN: 1-59532-483-6

First TOKYOPOP printing: December 2005

10 9 8 7 6 5 4 3 2 1

Printed in the U.S.A

Volume 3

So-Young Lee

HAMBURG // LONDON // LOS ANGELES // TOKYO

THE JOURNEY THUS FAR...

CHARGED WITH THE MISSION OF LOCATING A GUARDIAN DRAGON THAT WILL PROTECT HER KINGDOM, INEZ AND YULAN LEAVE THE WORLD OF MAN AND ENTER UNCHARTED TERRITORY. ALONG THE WAY, THEY ENCOUNTER MONG, A NYAMA–GENTLE CREATURES OF BOUNDLESS CURIOUSITY–AND KYRETTE, A HANDSOME MAN OF MYSTERY. WHEN THE GROUP STUMBLES ACROSS AN INJURED ELF NAMED ARIEL, INEZ FINDS HERSELF EMBROILED IN A ROYAL FAMILY FEUD. SOON, MATTERS BECOME EVEN MORE COMPLICATED WHEN POOR MONG IS CAPTURED BY THE RACE KNOWN AS THE BIG EARS!

ARCANA

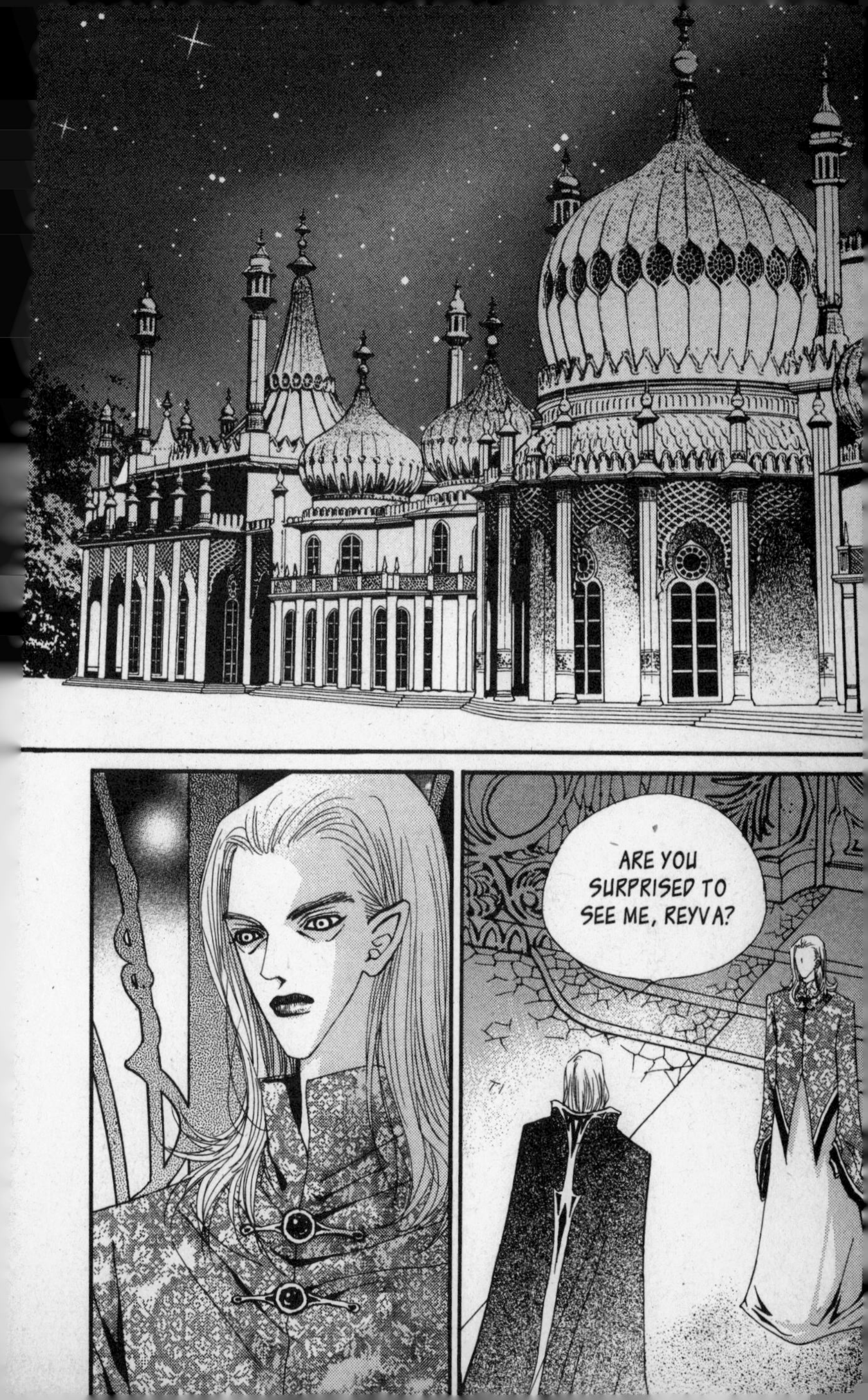
ARE YOU
SURPRISED TO
SEE ME, REYVA?

NO, OF COURSE NOT, LORD EZEKIEL. WHAT BRINGS YOU TO THIS SECTION OF THE EAST GARDEN...?

I WAS ADMIRING THE BEAUTY OF YOUR CASTLE.

ITS UNIQUE ARCHITECTURE LED MY EYE FROM ONE BUILDING TO THE NEXT.

I'M SORRY, IS THIS AREA OFF LIMITS?

NO, NOT AT ALL. HOW COULD ANYTHING BE OFF LIMITS TO YOU, LORD EZEKIEL?

IT'S JUST THAT...
...THESE ARE MY DAUGHTER'S QUARTERS. YOU SEE, SHE'S VERY ILL RIGHT NOW AND I'M TRYING TO KEEP HER FROM BEING DISTURBED.
SHE WAS BORN VERY FRAIL. I'VE TRIED TO GIVE HER EVERY TREATMENT UNDER THE SUN...
...BUT ELF MEDICINE SIMPLY CANNOT CURE HER CONDITION, IT SEEMS...
WITH YOUR PERMISSION, I WILL SEE IF THERE'S ANYTHING I CAN DO TO HELP YOUR DAUGHTER.

IN THIS COMATOSE STATE, I DON'T KNOW IF ANYTHING WILL WORK ON HER.
BUT HER TEMPERATURE AND PULSE SEEM NORMAL. AT LEAST HER LIFE IS NOT IN DANGER.
DID YOU...
...DO SOMETHING TO HER THAT YOU SHOULDN'T HAVE?
SHE'S SUSPENDED IN A FALSE SLEEP.

NO, LET ME PUT THAT QUESTION ANOTHER WAY.
I'M CURIOUS WHY YOU WOULD SHOW ME YOUR DAUGHTER SO READILY.
YOU DON'T STRIKE ME AS THE TYPE TO GIVE UP WITHOUT A FIGHT. I'M SURE YOU'VE GUESSED THAT IT WASN'T THE ARCHITECTURE THAT LED ME HERE.
A TRANSGRESSION OF THIS SERIOUSNESS DOES NOT RESULT IN A SIMPLE SLAP ON THE WRIST. YOU KNOW THAT.

I MUST CONFESS THAT YOUR AUDACITY IMPRESSES ME.

YOU DIDN'T TRY TO STOP ME FROM COMING IN HERE OR TO HIDE WHAT YOU HAVE DONE. WELL, I DON'T WANT TO INTERFERE IN YOUR PERSONAL BUSINESS, EITHER.

AS I'VE TOLD YOU, I CAME HERE TO ENJOY THE SCENERY, NOT TO KEEP AN EYE ON YOU. I CAN PRETEND THAT THE BEAUTIFUL SCENERY IS ALL I SAW HERE.

I AM, HOWEVER, CONCERNED ABOUT YOUR DAUGHTER.
WHAT WILL SHE THINK WHEN SHE FINDS OUT THAT HER FATHER'S RECKLESS ACT HAS CORRUPTED HER ESSENCE...?
WE ELVES LIVE A LONG TIME, PERHAPS FOREVER.
BUT ONLY IF OUR LIVES ARE KEPT AS PURE AS A CLEAR SPRING.
WE HAVE TO BE CAREFUL NOT TO TAINT OUR ESSENCE WITH EVEN THE SLIGHTEST IMPURITY.

THE MOMENT OUR INTERNAL ESSENCE IS CORRUPTED, THE LIGHT OF LIFE BEGINS TO FLICKER AND DWINDLE AWAY.

PLEASE, GET HIM OUT.
BREAK OPEN THE CAGE, KYRETTE, AND LET MONG OUT OF THERE.

PIECE OF CAKE. I WON'T EVEN NEED TO USE MY SWORD ON SOMETHING SO SIMPLE.
NO! DON'T BREAK IT!!
YOU'LL HURT THE NYAMA. THAT'S A MAGIC CAGE.
ONCE INSIDE, YOU CAN'T GET OUT UNLESS THE MAGIC SPELL IS UNDONE.
THE NYAMA IS FROZEN BECAUSE OF THE SPELL!

YOU MEAN MONG ISN'T DEAD?!
IF YOU BREAK THE CAGE NOW, THE NYAMA WILL DIE.
DID YOU JUST SAY...COLLECT?
WHAT DO YOU TAKE US FOR? BIG-EARS DON'T KILL.
WE DON'T USUALLY COLLECT LIVING CREATURES...
...BUT NYAMAS ARE SO RARE, WE COULDN'T RESIST.

GYAAAK... I CAN'T BREATHE!!
BRING MONG BACK! RIGHT NOW!!
COLLECT? COLLECT WHAT?!
LIVING BEINGS ARE NOT SOMETHING YOU CAN COLLECT!!
BUT WE DON'T HAVE THE KEY!

KOFF
THAT CAGE IS ELF-MADE.
KOFF
KOFF
WE WEREN'T ABLE TO GRAB THE KEY WHEN WE SMUGGLED THE CAGE OUT OF THE ELF-CASTLE.
WOW, HUMAN BEINGS ARE REALLY VIOLENT.
BUT WE CAN TAKE YOU TO WHERE THE KEY IS HIDDEN.

STRANGELY, THE SECURITY HERE IS MUCH LOOSER THAN ANYWHERE ELSE IN THE CASTLE.
WE STILL HAVE TO BE CAREFUL, THOUGH. ELVES HAVE SUPER-SENSITIVE EARS.
THE KEY IS INSIDE THAT ROOM.
BUT YOU'LL NEED A LOT OF LUCK TO BREAK THAT DOOR DOWN.

HOW DID YOU STEAL THE CAGE IN THE FIRST PLACE?
ONE DAY THE ELF STANDING GUARD FORGOT TO LOCK THE DOOR.
SO WE WENT IN... HOW COULD WE RESIST SUCH A GOLDEN OPPORTUNITY?
BUT HONESTLY, I DON'T EVER WANT TO GO BACK IN THERE AGAIN. I'VE NEVER SEEN A PLACE LIKE THAT.
WHAT AN INCREDIBLE PALACE!

KYRETTE, DO YOU THINK YOU COULD USE YOUR SWORD AGAIN?
NO, IT WON'T DO ANY GOOD TRYING TO REACH IT IN HERE. CAN'T YOU FEEL IT?
THE DARK ENERGY COMING FROM INSIDE.

YOUR FRIENDS?
THEY'RE NO LONGER HERE IN THE UNDERGROUND PASSAGE.
WE MUST GO UP INTO THE CASTLE, ARIEL.

...HA HA HA. I SEE NOTHING HAS CHANGED.
YULAN, YOU'RE TOO MORBID. GO FIND YOURSELF A SENSE OF HUMOR.
THAT PRICKLY PERSONALITY OF YOURS IS BEHIND ALL YOUR MISFORTUNES.
WELL, I GUESS YOUR LOWLY BIRTH DIDN'T HELP MATTERS ANY, HA HA HA.

BELIEVE IT OR NOT, I REALLY DON'T HAVE THE DESIRE TO LIVE MUCH LONGER. THANKS TO YOU, I'VE ENJOYED A VERY LONG LIFE.
YOU HAVE NOTHING TO GAIN BY PROVOKING ME, LONN.
AS YOU CAN SEE, I'M NEARLY BLIND NOW. I DON'T EVEN HAVE THE PLEASURE OF APPRECIATING THE VAST COLLECTION I'VE BUILT UP OVER THE YEARS. WHAT JOY IS THERE IN LIVING ANYMORE?
BUT MY EARS STILL FUNCTION. I CAN HEAR YOUR FRIENDS TALKING.
HA HA HA... THEY'RE WITH SOME OF MY KIDS.
THEY'RE ABOUT TO ENTER THE TREASURE CHAMBER.

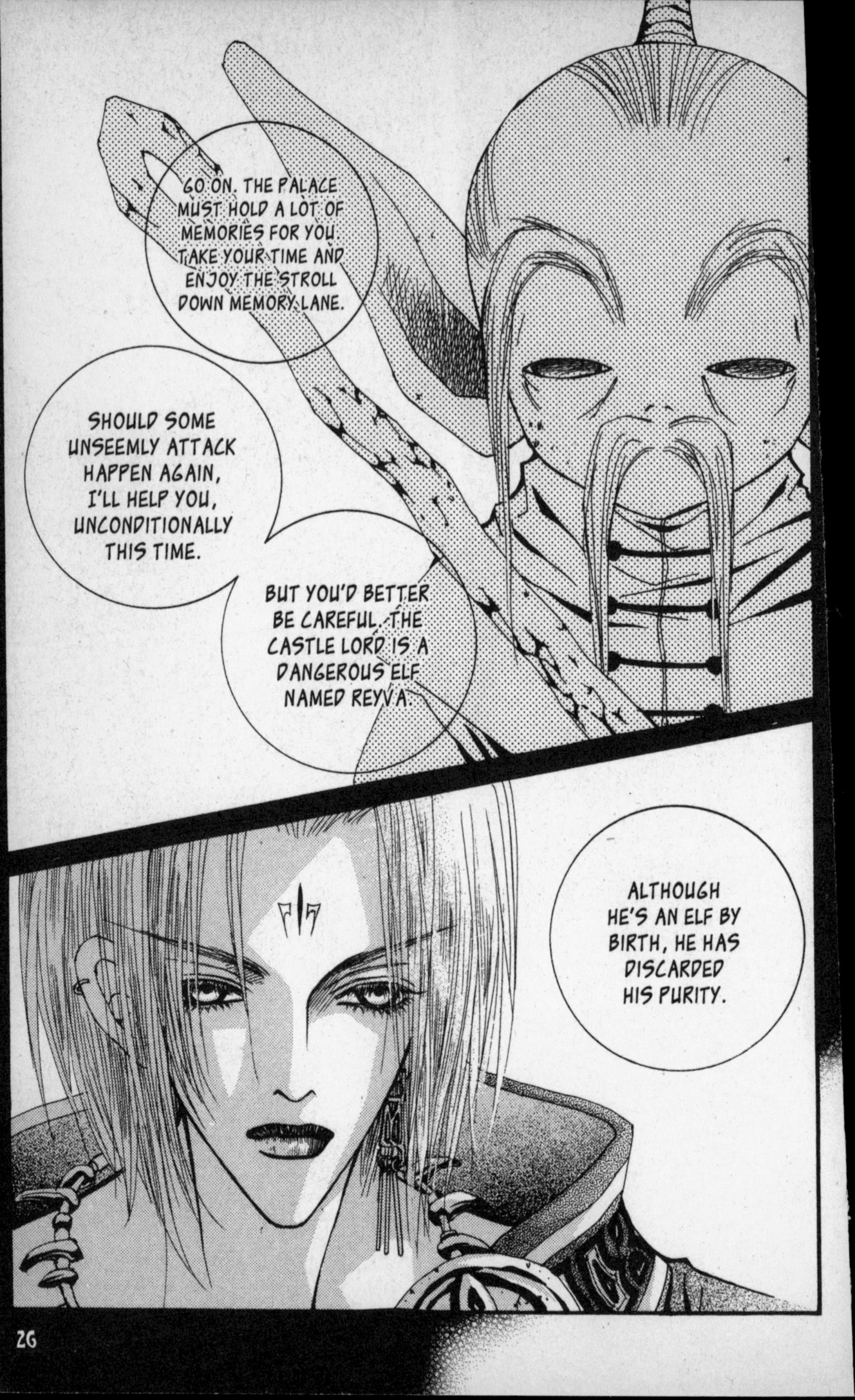
GO ON. THE PALACE MUST HOLD A LOT OF MEMORIES FOR YOU. TAKE YOUR TIME AND ENJOY THE STROLL DOWN MEMORY LANE.
SHOULD SOME UNSEEMLY ATTACK HAPPEN AGAIN, I'LL HELP YOU, UNCONDITIONALLY THIS TIME.
BUT YOU'D BETTER BE CAREFUL. THE CASTLE LORD IS A DANGEROUS ELF NAMED REYVA.
ALTHOUGH HE'S AN ELF BY BIRTH, HE HAS DISCARDED HIS PURITY.

BLACK
MAGIC?

I THINK SO. THIS DOOR'S BEEN BOLTED WITH A DARK MAGIC SPELL.
SOMEONE'S SEALED IT TIGHT FROM THE INSIDE.
FOR AN ELF TO USE BLACK MAGIC...
...IS A SERIOUSLY BAD THING.
IF MY HUNCH IS RIGHT, THE CASTLE LORD IS A VERY DANGEROUS ELF.

I NEVER KNEW THAT SUCH CREATURES LIVED RIGHT UNDER THE ELVES.

I'M SHOCKED THAT I NEVER ENCOUNTERED THEM BEFORE.

BUT NOW, THIS PLACE...

!

WHO WOULD DO SOMETHING THIS HORRIBLE...?
HOW DARE THEY DISTURB THE DEAD?
차랑

TAK
AN ELF! IS HE THE CASTLE LORD?

MY SWORD...
WHY WON'T IT APPEAR?

WHAT AN INTERESTING PLACE THIS IS.
ONE UNEXPECTED INCIDENT AFTER ANOTHER!
IS MY FACE THAT FRIGHTFUL?
YOU'RE ALL SHIVERING IN TERROR.
PLEASE, RELAX. I WON'T GOBBLE YOU UP, I PROMISE.
WHAT'S HE TALKING ABOUT? ISN'T HE THE LORD OF THIS CASTLE?

FOR SOME REASON, EVERYONE SEEMS TO BE TERRIBLY INTERESTED IN THIS SEALED CHAMBER.

BUT MAGIC IS NOT ALWAYS OMNIPOTENT.

A LOT DEPENDS ON THE STRENGTH OF THE MAGICIAN, AND EVEN THEN, HIS CONDITION AND HIS STATE OF MIND AFFECT THE SPELL.

UNFORTUNATELY, IT WON'T BE EASY TO GAIN ENTRANCE.

WOW! WHAT A WIND!
Whoosh
IT'S OPEN!

I GUESS HE ISN'T THE CASTLE LORD!
KYRETTE, LET'S GO INSIDE. THE DOOR'S OPEN.
KYRETTE?
꽉
FORGIVE ME FOR MAKING A SHOW OF MY POWER.
I WOULD LIKE TO TAKE A LOOK AROUND. HOW ABOUT ALL OF YOU?

MY SWORD WOULDN'T COME TO MY HAND.
WHAT... DOES THIS MEAN?

THE CAGE WAS OVER THERE. AND THE KEY WAS ON TOP...
AH, IT'S STILL THERE!
WHAT CREEPY THINGS!
DISGUSTING.
GREAT. NOW THAT WE HAVE THE KEY, LET'S GET OUT OF HERE.

TAKE THE FLASK.
KYRETTE, LET'S GO! WE HAVE THE KEY.

AREN'T THERE ANY OTHER EXITS?
THERE MUST BE ONE! WE JUST HAVE TO LOOK HARDER.
EVEN IF THERE IS ONE, IT'S BOUND TO BE SEALED.
WE CAN'T.
Whooosh
NOT UNLESS WE USE THE SAME MAGIC THE ELF USED.

KRAK
WAIT!
I KNEW IT! THIS WAS A TRAP TO LOCK US IN!
BANG
BANG
I KNEW IT COULDN'T BE THIS EASY.
NO.
WHAT GOOD IS FINDING THE KEY IF WE CAN'T GET OUT OF HERE?

IF HE WANTED TO LOCK US IN...
...HE WOULDN'T BE SHOWING US THE WAY OUT.
HE SEEMS TO BE LEADING US SOMEWHERE.

I'M NOT A HUNDRED PERCENT SURE ABOUT THIS, BUT I DON'T THINK THIS IS A TRAP.
AN ELF THIS POWERFUL WOULDN'T GO TO ALL THIS TROUBLE JUST TO LURE US.
HE COULD GET RID OF US IN A BLINK IF HE WANTED TO.
HE CAN BLOCK MY SWORD.
WE HAVE NO CHOICE, ANYWAY. THIS IS OUR ONLY WAY OUT.
LEAD THE WAY.

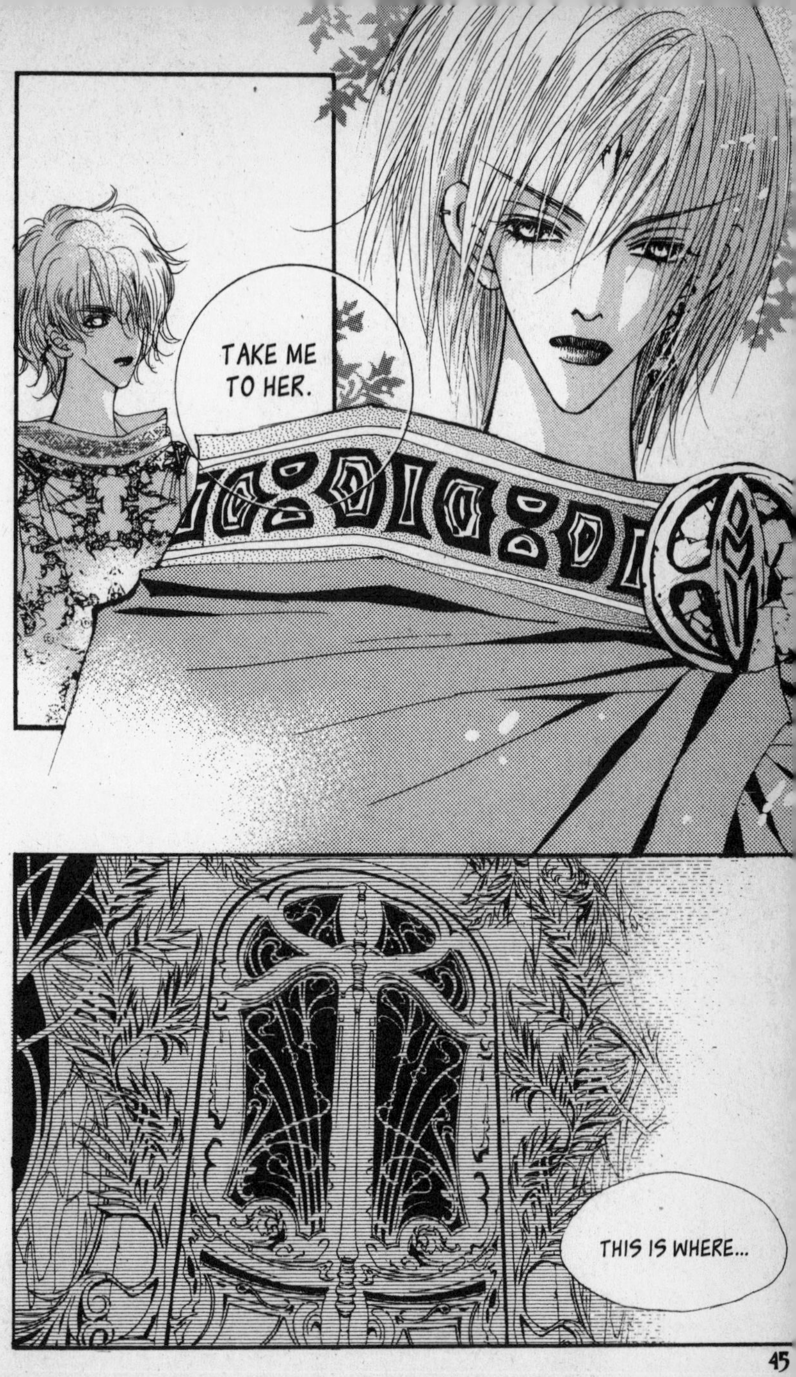
TAKE ME TO HER.
THIS IS WHERE...

...THE ELF LORD'S DAUGHTER IS KEPT.
SHE MUST BE THE ONE WE'RE TRYING TO RESCUE-- REANA.
YEAH, REANA IS HER NAME. HOW DID YOU KNOW THAT?
SHE'S THE MOST BEAUTIFUL ELF I'VE EVER LAID MY EYES ON. BUT SHE DOESN'T STEP A FOOT OUTSIDE THAT ROOM ANYMORE.
WE CAME ACROSS HER IN THE GARDEN ONE DAY. INSTEAD OF BEING SURPRISED...
...SHE GAVE US THE MOST DAZZLING SMILE.

KYRETTE, DON'T YOU THINK IT'S WEIRD? IT'S ALMOST AS IF THAT ELF WANTED TO LEAD US RIGHT TO HER ROOM.
LIKE HE KNEW WHY WE CAME HERE IN THE FIRST PLACE.
WHO WAS THAT ELF?
I HAVE A STRANGE FEELING.
THAT SOMETHING'S LOCKED UP BEHIND THAT DOOR.
WHAT FEELING?

STRENGTHEN SECURITY AROUND THE CASTLE, ESPECIALLY NEAR THE INNER QUARTERS. NO, NEVER MIND. I'LL TEND TO THAT MYSELF.
...WHY IS IT SUDDENLY SO QUIET? I CAN'T EVEN READ THE DIRECTION OF THE WIND ANYMORE... COULD SOMEONE HAVE CAST...
...A SPELL?

SO HERE YOU ARE, LORD REYVA.
MAYBE IT'S BECAUSE OF THE WONDROUS SCENERY IN THIS PLACE THAT I CAN'T FIND SLEEP.
AH...
I CAN'T SENSE A THING. THIS MUST BE A SPELL.
BUT IF IT IS, THERE'S ONLY ONE PERSON WHO COULD HAVE CAST IT...

...IS SHE SLEEPING?
NO, SHE'S UNDER A SPELL. IT ONLY LOOKS LIKE SHE'S SLEEPING.

ARE YOU SAYING THAT THE CASTLE LORD DID THIS TO HIS OWN DAUGHTER?
SHE'S AS GOOD AS DEAD! WHY WOULD HE DO SOMETHING LIKE THAT?
BECAUSE SHE LOVED A HALF-ELF.
WHAT?
HALF-ELVES ARE CONSIDERED SLAVES AMONG ELVES. FOR A HALF-ELF TO LOVE AN ARISTOCRAT IS A SERIOUS OFFENSE.
THE CASTLE LORD PROBABLY THOUGHT THAT THIS WAS THE BEST WAY TO SEPARATE THE YOUNG LOVERS. I SUPPOSE KILLING THE HALF-ELF WOULD HAVE BEEN ANOTHER OPTION...
BUT SOMETIMES LOVE SURVIVES EVEN DEATH.

THAT'S RIDICULOUS. HOW COULD STATUS BE AN OBSTACLE TO TRUE LOVE?
WOULD THE CASTLE LORD RATHER SEE HIS DAUGHTER ALMOST DEAD THAN HAPPY IN LOVE?
NO NEED GETTING ALL RILED UP.
JUST LIKE HUMAN SOCIETY, ELF SOCIETY IS STATUS-BASED. YOUR BIRTH DETERMINES YOUR ENTIRE LIFE.
ELVES CONSIDER HUMAN BEINGS AN INFERIOR RACE.
NATURALLY, THEN, THEY WOULD CONSIDER A HALF-ELF WITH HUMAN BLOOD TO BE BENEATH THEM.

BUT...

THE HUMAN RACE HAS BEEN THE MOST HATED IN ALL OF HISTORY. BUT ALL THOSE RACES THAT COMPLAIN ABOUT HUMANITY'S CRUELTY...

...CAN THEY PARDON THEMSELVES FOR BEING JUST AS CORRUPT AS THOSE THEY HATE?

YOU TALK AS IF HUMAN BEINGS ACT ANY DIFFERENTLY.

A SLAVE IS NO LESS FREE TO LOVE A PRINCESS IN HUMAN SOCIETY.

KYRETTE...
THERE'S SO MUCH HATRED IN HIM.
SO MUCH HOSTILITY, JUST LIKE YULAN.
BUT WHO...IS IT AIMED AT?
WHAT IS THIS FEELING?
THIS FAMILIAR SENSE OF RAGE?

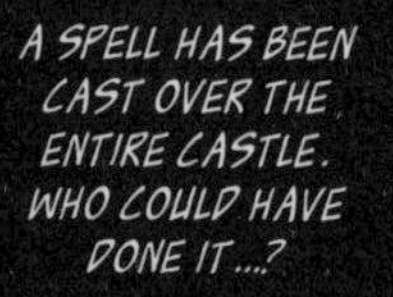
A SPELL HAS BEEN CAST OVER THE ENTIRE CASTLE. WHO COULD HAVE DONE IT...?
ONLY A FEW ELVES WOULD BE POWERFUL ENOUGH...

COULD IT BE HIM?
NO, IT CAN'T BE. HE WOULD NEVER COME BACK HERE AGAIN.
HE HAS ALREADY TAKEN EVERYTHING HE COULD FROM THIS PLACE.

THAT ROOM IS WHERE REANA LIES.
HMM, THERE'S NO SPELL OVER THIS PLACE...

EXCUSE ME, LORD EZEKIEL.
THERE IS A MATTER I MUST TEND TO.
HOW RUDE.
THIS IS THE SECOND TIME TODAY YOU'VE COMMITTED SUCH A BREACH OF ETIQUETTE.
I SUPPOSE I MUST SHARE THE BLAME FOR THIS.
IT SEEMS YOU DON'T CARE TO SPEND TIME WITH ME. I CAN'T SAY THAT IT PLEASES ME TO BE TREATED THIS WAY.
I THOUGHT I MADE IT CLEAR THAT I WILL PRETEND THAT I SAW NOTHING OUT OF THE ORDINARY HERE.

OF ALL THE DIFFERENT MAGIC SPELLS, BLACK MAGIC ONES HAVE TO BE THE MOST PERFECT, THE MOST FLAWLESS.
THE MORE SERIOUS A SPELL'S IMPERFECTIONS...
BUT THERE IS ONE THING YOU MUST KEEP IN MIND.
I BEG YOUR FORGIVENESS.
DO AS YOU PLEASE.
...THE GREATER THE DAMAGE TO THE SPELL-CASTER ONCE IT'S BROKEN.
I'M SURE YOU WERE PERFECTLY AWARE OF THIS WHEN YOU CAST YOURS.

REANA!

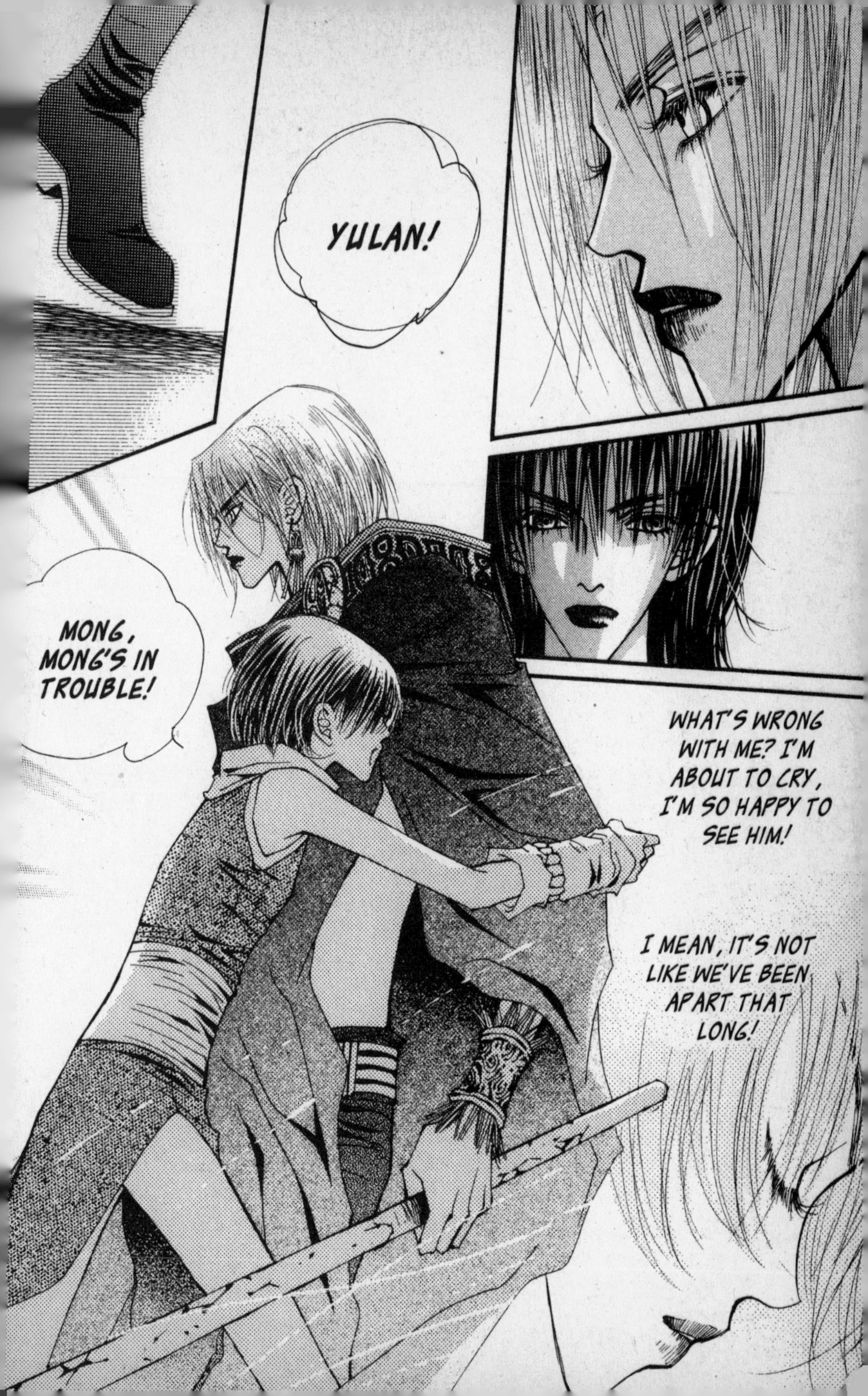
YULAN!
MONG, MONG'S IN TROUBLE!
WHAT'S WRONG WITH ME? I'M ABOUT TO CRY, I'M SO HAPPY TO SEE HIM!
I MEAN, IT'S NOT LIKE WE'VE BEEN APART THAT LONG!

HEY, KID, DON'T YOU THINK YOU'RE OVERDOING IT A BIT?
AND PEOPLE MIGH START GETTING THE WRONG IDEA ABOUT YOU TWO.
DON'T MAKE IT LOOK LIKE I MISTREATED YOU.
YULAN'S NEVER LOOKED AT ME WITH AN OUNCE OF TENDERNESS...
NEVER SAID A WORD TO SHOW HE CARES...
I DON'T UNDERSTAND MY OWN REACTION. IS IT REALLY ME ACTING THIS WAY?
PEEK
YEAH, THERE WAS SOMETHING UNNATURAL ABOUT THE WHOLE THING JUST NOW.
I MUST HAVE GONE NUTS, COMPLETELY NUTS!

YULAN!
UMM... NOTHING. NEVER MIND.
THERE'S SOMETHING I WANT TO SAY TO YOU... BUT NOT RIGHT NOW.
BUT SOMEDAY...
BUT FIRST, WE SHOULD CONCLUDE THIS OTHER BUSINESS.
DON'T WORRY ABOUT MONG. HE'LL BE FINE, NOW THAT YOU'VE FOUND THE KEY.
OH! YOU KNEW ABOUT IT?
HE KNOWS EVERYTHING.

ARIEL, ARE YOU MY SLAVE?

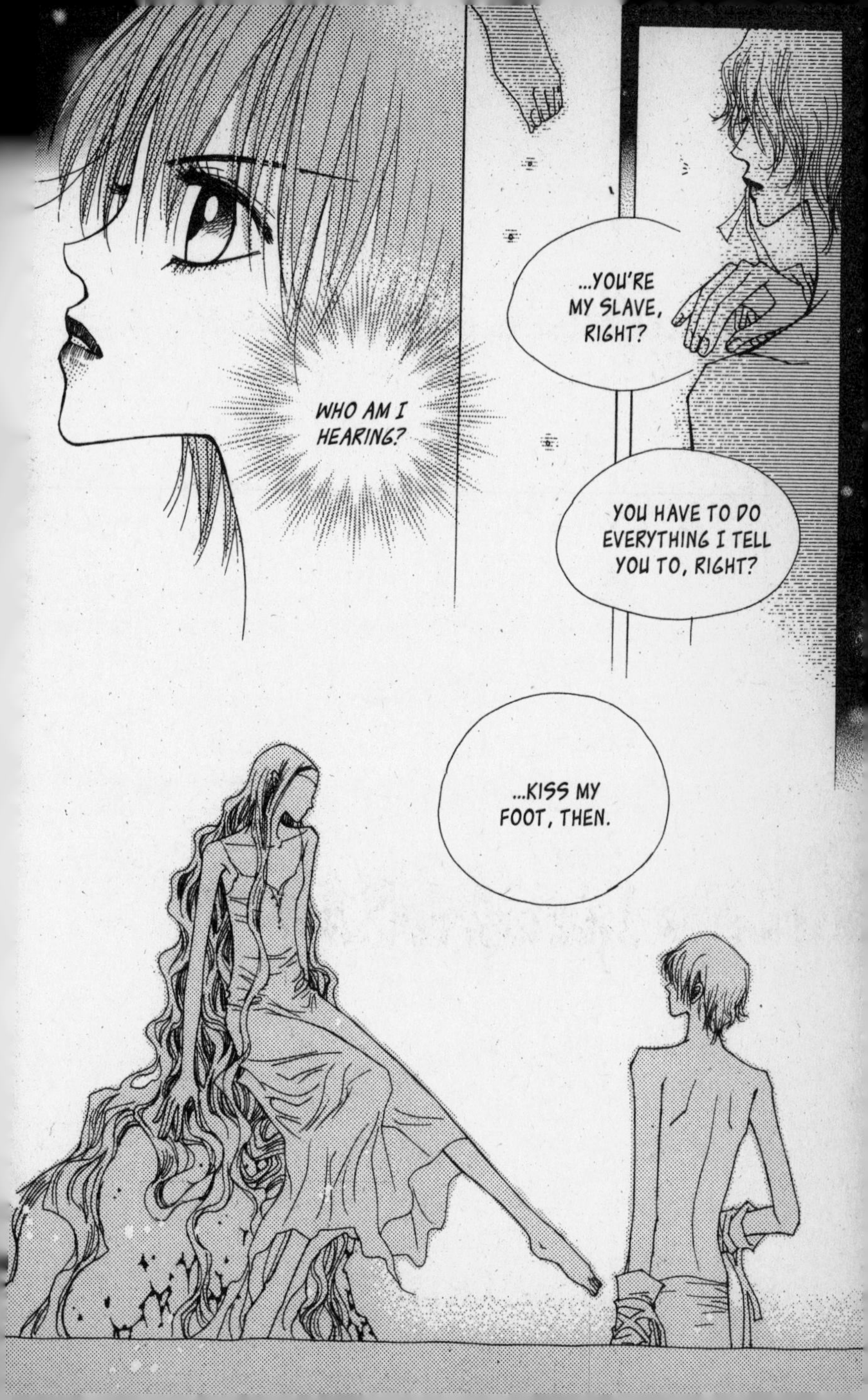
...YOU'RE MY SLAVE, RIGHT?
WHO AM I HEARING?
YOU HAVE TO DO EVERYTHING I TELL YOU TO, RIGHT?
...KISS MY FOOT, THEN.

SWEAR TO ME...
SWEAR BY THAT KISS, ARIEL.
THAT WE'LL NEVER...
...NEVER...

...GIVE EACH
OTHER UP.

HOW DARE YOU?!
HOW DARE YOU?!
PROMISE ME, ARIEL, THAT YOU'LL NEVER GIVE ME UP.
HOW DARE YOU SULLY MY DAUGHTER?!

WHERE ARE YOU, INEZ...?
I'LL NEVER FEEL GREATER PAIN...
...THAN WHEN YOU LEAVE ME...

REANA'S SORROW FLOODS MY HEART.
IF YOU NEVER LOVE, THEN YOU'LL NEVER SUFFER PAIN.
NO... IT ISN'T REANA'S SORROW ANYMORE.
RIGHT, YULAN?

IF YOU GIVE UP LOVING ANOTHER, THEN THE CYCLE OF PAIN ALSO COMES TO AN END.
IF YOU DON'T LOVE ANYONE...
THEN, WHOSE?
...LOVE NO ONE, YOU'LL BE FREE FROM PAIN...?

...AN AURA?
THERE'S AN AURA EMANATING FROM THEM.
IT'S BEGINNING AGAIN!
WHOSE AURA? YULAN'S? OR IS IT...
...NO!

IF YOU'VE COME HERE TO RESCUE REANA, SMUGGLE HER OUT AND BRING HER DOWN TO WHERE WE LIVE.
BIG-EARS LIVE UNDERGROUND, AND ELVES HATE BEING UNDERGROUND.
NO, WE CAN'T DO THAT. UNLESS THE SPELL IS UNDONE BEFORE WE LEAVE THE CASTLE, REANA WON'T EVER WAKE UP.
SO WHAT DO WE DO, THEN?
PLEASE, NOT THIS TIME!

THAT'S OBVIOUS, ISN'T IT? EITHER FIND A WAY TO UNDO THE SPELL, OR KILL THE SPELLCASTER.
I SAY THE LATTER'S INFINITELY EASIER.
AFTER ALL, YOU CAN'T VERY WELL ASK HIM NICELY TO UNDO THE SPELL.
IF KILLING HIM WOULD SOLVE THE PROBLEM, THERE'D BE NOTHING TO WORRY ABOUT.
BUT THE MAGIC SPELL THE PRINCESS LIES UNDER IS BLACK MAGIC. KILLING THE SPELL-CASTER WON'T FREE HER.
SO SHE'LL SLEEP FOREVER?

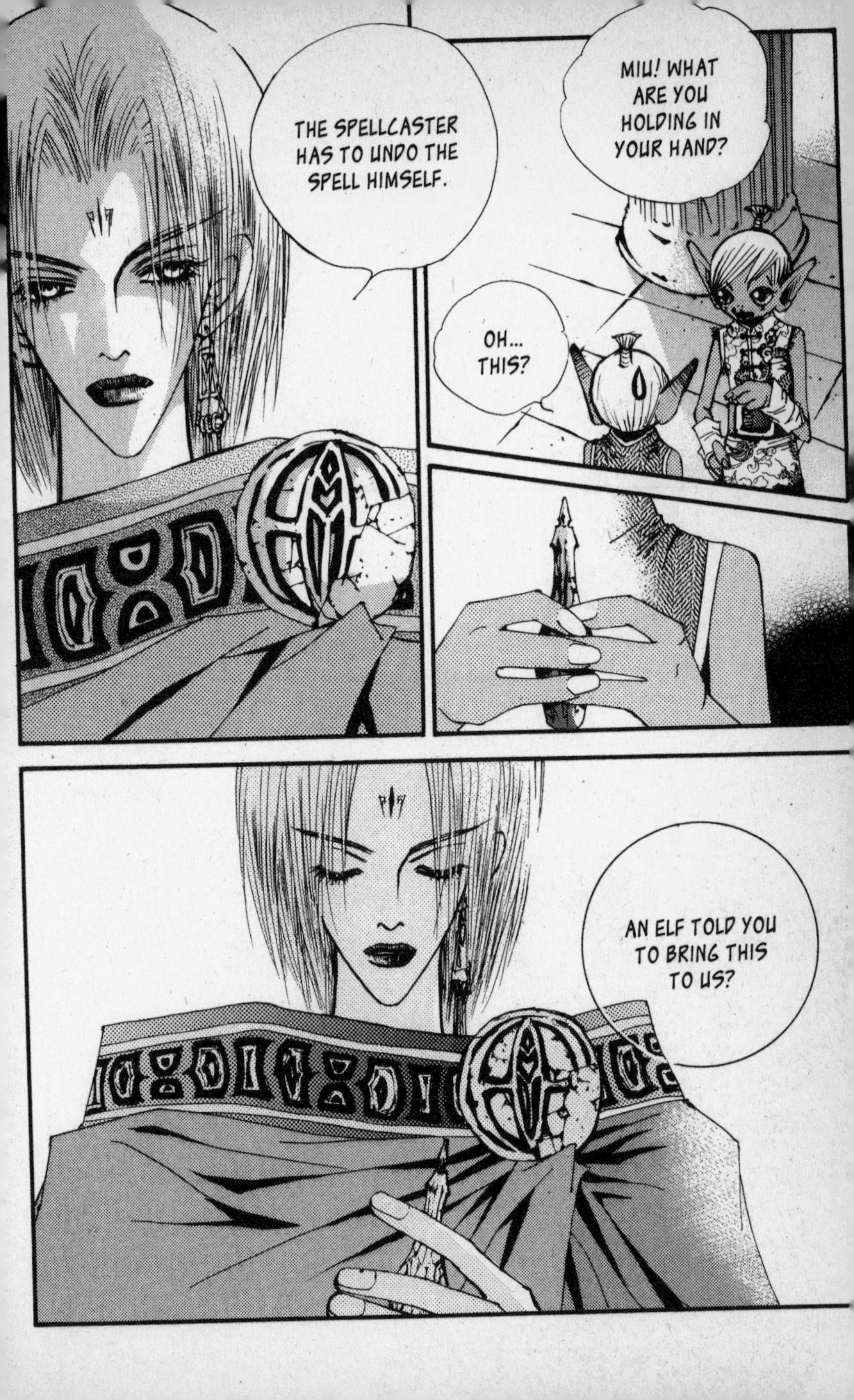
THE SPELLCASTER HAS TO UNDO THE SPELL HIMSELF.
MIU! WHAT ARE YOU HOLDING IN YOUR HAND?
OH... THIS?
AN ELF TOLD YOU TO BRING THIS TO US?

HE DIDN'T SAY THAT IN SO MANY WORDS, BUT THAT'S THE FEELING I GOT.
WHAT IS IT ANYWAY?
SOMEONE IS TRYING TO HELP US? WHY?
WHO?
ARIEL, MOVE REANA SOMEWHERE SAFER.
BUT MAKE SURE YOU DON'T MOVE HER TOO FAR AWAY FROM HERE.
AS FOR YOU...
NO WAY--I DON'T WANT TO!! NO, I DON'T WANT TO!!

HMM, I WONDER WHICH DRESS WILL FIT YOU THE BEST?
THIS IS CRAZY! WHY DO I HAVE TO DO THIS?
YOU HAVE NO MANNERS!!
LET ME GO. I WANT TO GO HOME!
바둥 바둥
STOP WHINING AND LOOK ON THE BRIGHT SIDE. THIS IS ALL FOR REANA. DIDN'T YOU SAY YOU LIKED HER?
WE HAVE TO HURRY. THE ELF-LORD WILL BE HERE ANY MINUTE NOW.
NOOO--!!
I'LL DO IT.

I'LL PRETEND TO BE REANA.
AH! THAT'S A GREAT IDEA!

HEY, KID--IT'S NOT TOO LATE TO CHANGE YOUR MIND. YOU COULD GET KILLED.
NO, I'M DOING IT.
THE ELF-LORD HAS A LOT OF POWER.
SO YOU MEAN YOU WERE GOING TO MAKE ME A SITTING DUCK FOR THIS POWERFUL WIZARD!
!
......
MM MM...
NO.
NOTHING BAD WILL HAPPEN.

I HAVE FAITH IN YULAN.

THIS IS A SPECIAL POTION. MIX IT WITH ASHES FROM SOMEONE'S HAIR, DRINK IT, AND YOU'LL LOOK, SPEAK, ACT, EVEN SMILE LIKE THAT PERSON.
I'VE ALREADY MIXED ASHES FROM REANA'S HAIR INTO IT.

HEY, KID--LAST CHANCE TO CHANGE YOUR MIND. THINK BEFORE YOU DIVE INTO THIS.
NO, THIS IS SOMETHING I STARTED. I CAN'T LET SOMEONE ELSE TAKE THE RESPONSIBILITY.
WITH ALL MY HEART...
I WANT TO HELP THEM.

I'M GOING INSIDE. ALONE.
WAIT OUT HERE.

WAS IT JUST THE WEATHER? THERE'S NO SENSE OF A SPELL ON THIS PLACE ANYMORE. DID EZEKIEL CAST A SPELL AND THEN DISABLE IT?

IF SO, WHY? WHAT IS HE HIDING? DIDN'T HE TELL ME THAT HE WON'T EXPOSE WHAT I'VE BEEN DOING HERE?

EZEKIEL, WHAT ARE YOU UP TO?

sroosh

REANA? HOW DID YOU...?
I CAN'T BELIEVE IT! MY SPELL...

WHAT'S HAPPENED TO MY SPELL?
IT'S NOT THE KIND OF MAGIC THAT JUST GETS BROKEN.
SOMEONE HAS DONE SOMETHING...
ISN'T THIS WHAT YOU WANTED?
WHO'S THERE?

BY CASTING THE MAGIC SPELL, YOU WANTED TO PLUNGE YOUR DAUGHTER INTO A COMA...
...AND SLOWLY ERODE HER MEMORY.
BUT MAGIC IS FRAGILE BY NATURE.
AND YOUR POWER IS NOT GREAT ENOUGH TO WIELD BLACK MAGIC.
YOU INTENDED TO ERASE HER MEMORY, BUT ENDED UP IMPRISONING HER SOUL.
SO SHE HAS BECOME A LIVING DOLL, BREATHING BUT UNCONSCIOUS...
I ASSUME YOU WANTED TO KEEP HER BY YOUR SIDE, EVEN IF IT MEANT REDUCING HER TO AN EMPTY SHELL.

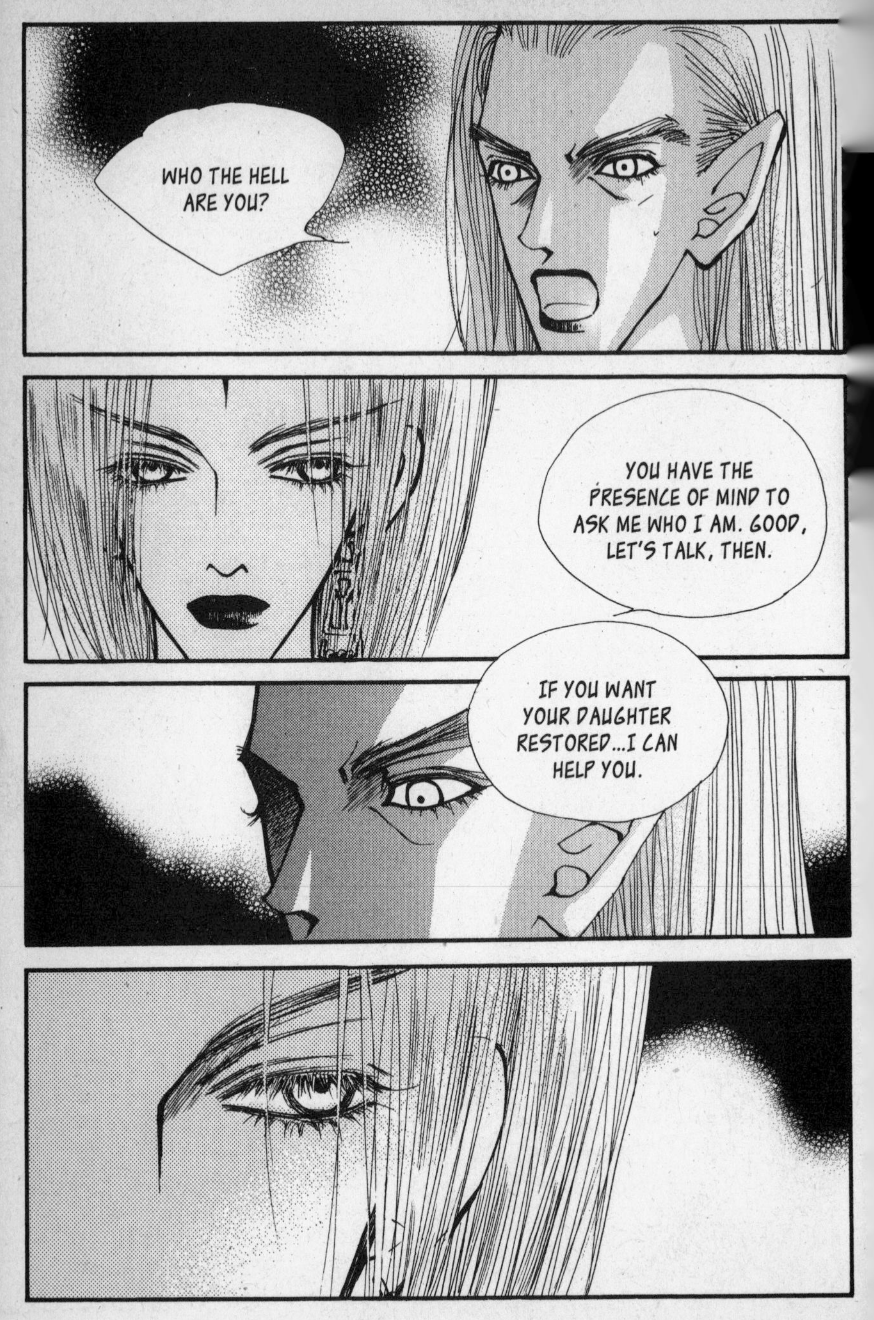
WHO THE HELL ARE YOU?
YOU HAVE THE PRESENCE OF MIND TO ASK ME WHO I AM. GOOD, LET'S TALK, THEN.
IF YOU WANT YOUR DAUGHTER RESTORED...I CAN HELP YOU.

TO GET HER BACK THE WAY SHE WAS, NOT AS A LIVING DOLL, BUT THE LOVELY DAUGHTER YOU ONCE KNEW...
...FIRST UNDO THE SPELL YOU CAST ON HER.
HER COMPLETE RESTORATION WILL TAKE MANY MORE STEPS...
...COMPLICATED MEASURES TO COUNTERACT THE DAMAGE YOU'VE DONE.
BUT OPENING THAT FIRST LOCK IS YOUR RESPONSIBILITY.

FINE.
I'M WILLING.
BUT HOW CAN I TRUST THE WORD OF A COMPLETE STRANGER? I DON'T EVEN KNOW WHO YOU ARE.
ISN'T THAT PROOF ENOUGH?
YOU FELT THE EFFECT OF A SPELL SURROUNDING THE ENTIRE CASTLE, DIDN'T YOU?
REYVA, I KNOW YOU CAME HERE BECAUSE YOU SENSED THAT MAGIC.

IS HE THE ONE... RESPONSIBLE FOR THAT SPELL?
IF HE IS, HIS POWER EQUALS THAT OF EZEKIEL, THE HIGH ELF AND GRAND WIZARD.
CLENCH
I HAVE ONE MORE QUESTION. WHY DO YOU WANT TO HELP ME?
WHAT DO YOU GET OUT OF THIS?
LET'S JUST SAY THAT A FRIEND ASKED ME FOR A FAVOR.

A FRIEND...?
I CAN PRETEND THAT THE BEAUTIFUL SCENERY IS ALL I SAW HERE.
I CAME ALL THIS WAY LOOKING FOR A FRIEND TO TALK TO.
COULD THAT FRIEND BE...?
NOW EVERYTHING IS FALLING INTO PLACE.
EZEKIEL SAID THAT HE'S HERE TO ENJOY THE SCENERY, BUT HE'S HERE TO KEEP AN EYE ON ME AFTER ALL!
EZEKIEL?

NO FATHER WANTS TO LOCK HIS BLOOD DAUGHTER AWAY FOR ETERNITY.
I USED THE SPELL OF FORGETFULNESS TO ERASE THE STAIN CAUSED BY MY DAUGHTER'S MISBEGOTTEN LOVE AFFAIR.
ALL THAT TALK ABOUT KEEPING THINGS SECRET WAS PART OF HIS TRAP!
NOW THAT HE KNOWS I'VE DIRTIED MY HANDS WITH BLACK MAGIC, HE WON'T JUST SIT IDLY BY AND DO NOTHING.
MY POWER IS NOT STRONG NOUGH TO GO UP AGAINST HIM BY MYSELF. I FIRST HAVE TO FIGURE OUT JUST WHAT HE'S AFTER.

BUT I WISH MORE THAN ANYTHING TO BE ABLE TO RETURN MY DAUGHTER TO THE WAY SHE WAS.

I LOVE YOU, REANA...
......
AMAZING. YOU ALMOST HAD ME FOOLED.

FROM HEAD TO TOE, SHE LOOKS EXACTLY LIKE REANA.
WHAT MAGIC POTION DID YOU USE TO GIVE HER MY DAUGHTER'S SCENT?
NEARLY PERFECT, BUT NOT PERFECT ENOUGH. YOU COULDN'T DISGUISE A MINUT TREMBLING OF THE LIPS.
A DOLL WOULDN'T TREMBLE LIKE THAT, NOW WOULD IT?

HAVE I BEEN... CAUGHT?
NOW IT'S MY TURN TO FIGURE OUT...
...HOW BEST TO ENJOY THIS EAUTIFUL DOLL.
I SUPPOSE THEY WOULD CALL THIS A SURPRISE TWIST.
IT'D BE A SHAME TO DESTROY SOMETHING SO PERFECT.
squeeze

WHAT THE HELL IS ALL THIS?!
YOU DARE TRY TO TRICK ME?
BRING MY DAUGHTER BACK THIS INSTANT!!
I... I CAN'T BREATHE!

Kranng
LORD REYVA!
YOU...!
PLEASE, I BEG F YOU, PLEASE. LET REANA GO!
LORD REYVA, SHE WAS YOUR DAUGHTER BEFORE SHE EVER BECAME MY LOVE.
PLEASE DON'T LET REANA REMAIN IN ETERNAL DARKNESS.
IF YOU MUST, TAKE MY LIFE... BUT LET HER LIVE!

NOW I UNDERSTAND WHAT'S GOING ON. ALL OF THIS IS A PLOT YOU COOKED UP!
MAYBE YOU SOLD YOUR FILTHY BODY TO GET THEM TO HELP YOU.
BUT YOU WON'T HAVE YOUR WAY WITH MY DAUGHTER EVER AGAIN!
YOU *DARE?*
DO YOU PRESUME THAT YOUR LIFE COULD BE EXCHANGED FOR MY DAUGHTER'S? THAT THEY'RE OF EQUAL VALUE?
IT MAKES NO DIFFERENCE TO ME WHAT HAPPENS TO YOUR PATHETIC LITTLE LIFE!
BUT I WOULD RATHER KEEP MY DAUGHTER BY MY SIDE AS SHE IS NOW THAN TO WATCH HER BEFOUL HERSELF WITH YOU!
LORD REYVA!

I AM THE ONE WHO GAVE REANA HER LIFE.
IF I SO WISH, IT IS MY PREROGATIVE...
...TO TAKE THAT LIFE BACK.

NO! REANA!
NOOOO!!

NOOO!
Drip

GIRRK

GAK
REANA...

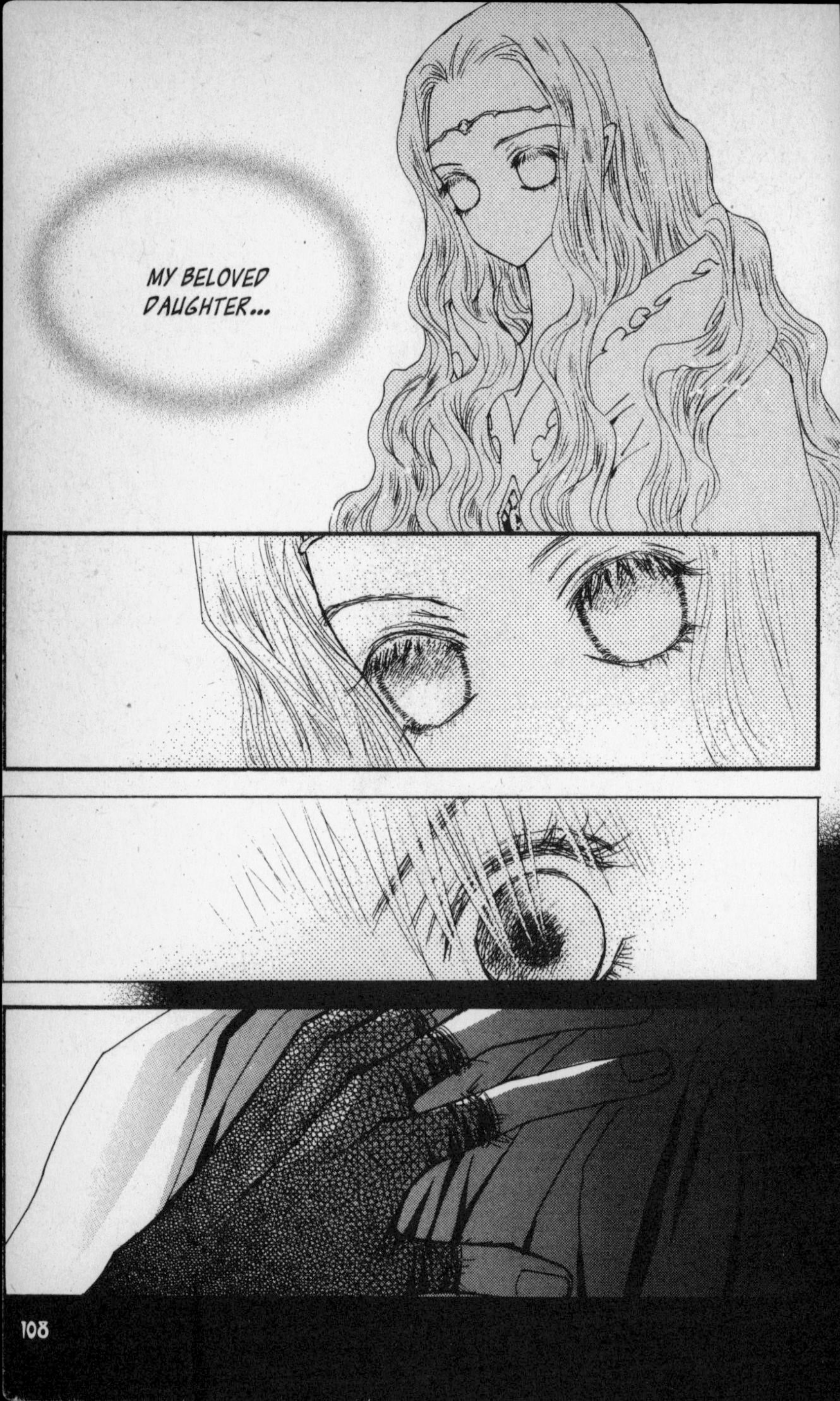
MY BELOVED
DAUGHTER...

EVERYTHING...

...HAPPENED SO QUICKLY...
KYRETTE...?

NO!

TIME YOU WOKE UP! HOW COULD YOU SLEEP STRAIGHT THROUGH FOR TWO WHOLE DAYS?
AREN'T YOU HUNGRY?
KYRETTE!!

MONG!
MONG!
와락
WE BROUGHT HIM HERE WHILE YOU WERE SLEEPING.
HE WAS SO WORRIED ABOUT YOU, HE WOULDN'T EVEN EAT.
MONG, PROMISE ME YOU'LL ALWAYS STAY BY MY SIDE FROM NOW ON.
I'M SORRY I COULDN'T DO A BETTER JOB OF PROTECTING YOU. I'LL NEVER LET ANYTHING HURT YOU AGAIN...

EAST GARDEN... AN UNASSUMING NAME, BUT THE PLACE HAS SEEN SO MANY TRAGEDIES.
IT'S LOST ITS MASTER ONCE AGAIN.
WHO ARE YOU? WHY DID YOU HELP US?
BY THE WAY, YOU KNOW THAT GUY NAMED KYRETTE...?
!

NO, YOU'RE THE ONES WHO HELPED US. WE DIDN'T WANT TO BE THE ONES TO KILL ONE OF OUR OWN.
WHETHER OR NOT THE SPELL BINDING HIS DAUGHTER'S LIFE COULD BE REMOVED, REYVA WAS AT THE END OF HIS ROPE...
...AND THANKS TO YOU, THAT ROPE IS NOW BROKEN.
TO MAINTAIN ORDER IN ELF SOCIETY, OBSTACLES MUST BE REMOVED FROM TIME TO TIME.
TODAY WAS ONE SUCH INSTANCE. YOU MIGHT SAY THAT WE BORROWED YOUR HANDS TO DO OUR SPRING-CLEANING.

AND I SEEK YOUR FORGIVENESS FOR PEERING INTO YOUR COLLEAGUE'S HEART TO GATHER SOME MUCH-NEEDED INFORMATION.
YOU...HAVE BEAUTIFUL EYES.
ching
kranng
I WOULDN'T TRY ANYTHING LIKE THAT IF I WERE YOU.

EYES OF RARE BEAUTY, EVEN AMONG THE ELVES.
IT'S A SHAME THAT THEY HAVE LOST THEIR LUSTER.
BUT HOW COULD I NOT BE DRAWN TO...
...THE POSSESSOR OF SUCH EYES?

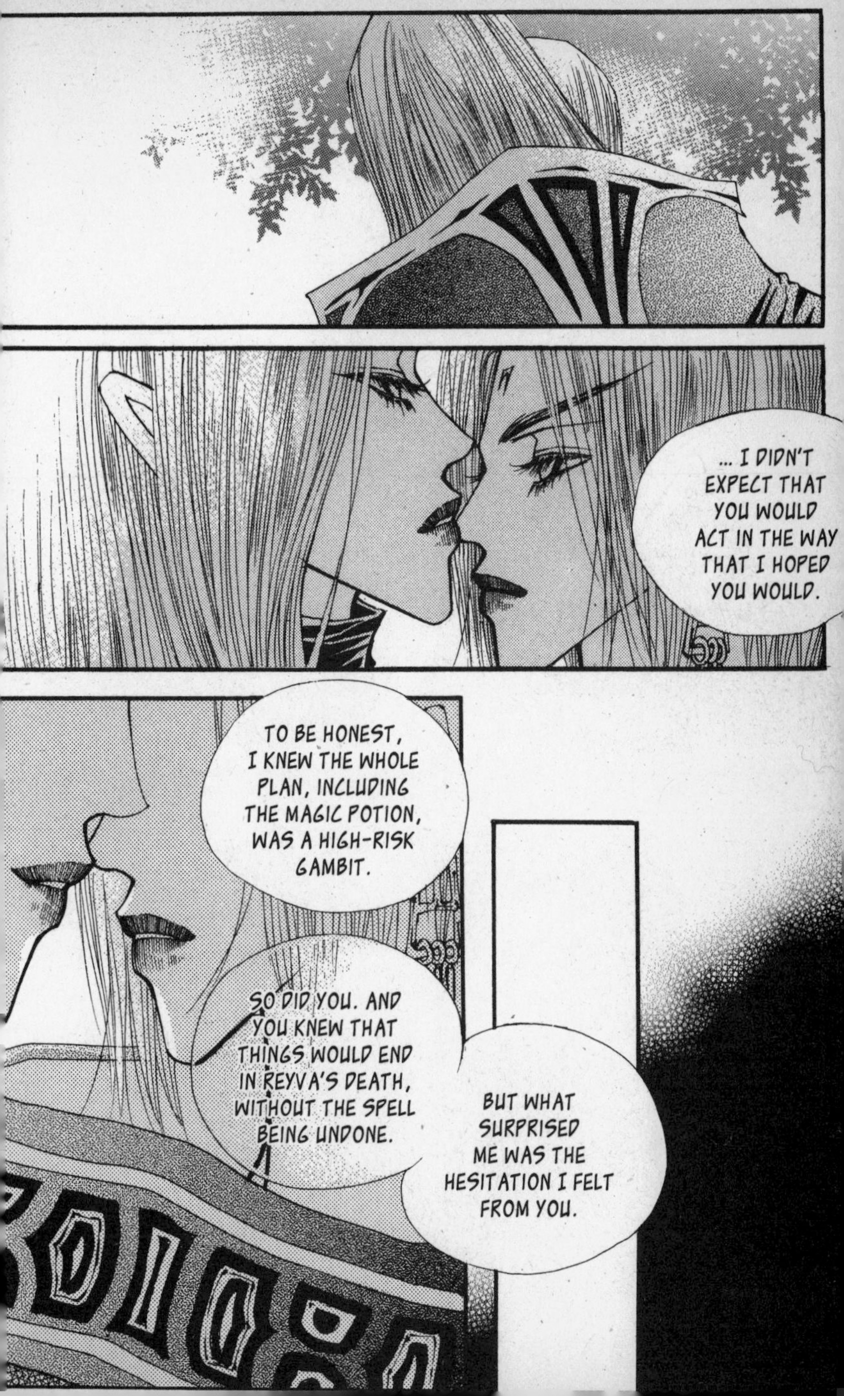

... I DIDN'T EXPECT THAT YOU WOULD ACT IN THE WAY THAT I HOPED YOU WOULD.
TO BE HONEST, I KNEW THE WHOLE PLAN, INCLUDING THE MAGIC POTION, WAS A HIGH-RISK GAMBIT.
SO DID YOU. AND YOU KNEW THAT THINGS WOULD END IN REYVA'S DEATH, WITHOUT THE SPELL BEING UNDONE.
BUT WHAT SURPRISED ME WAS THE HESITATION I FELT FROM YOU.

EAST GARDEN... I WONDER WHO WILL BE ITS MASTER NOW.

HUKh

HUKh

NO ONE WILL EVER KNOW...

HUKh

HUKh

...HOW MUCH YOU HESITATED.

HOW MUCH...

I HAVE FAITH IN YULAN.
쾅
I...
...HAVE FAITH IN YULAN.
콰광

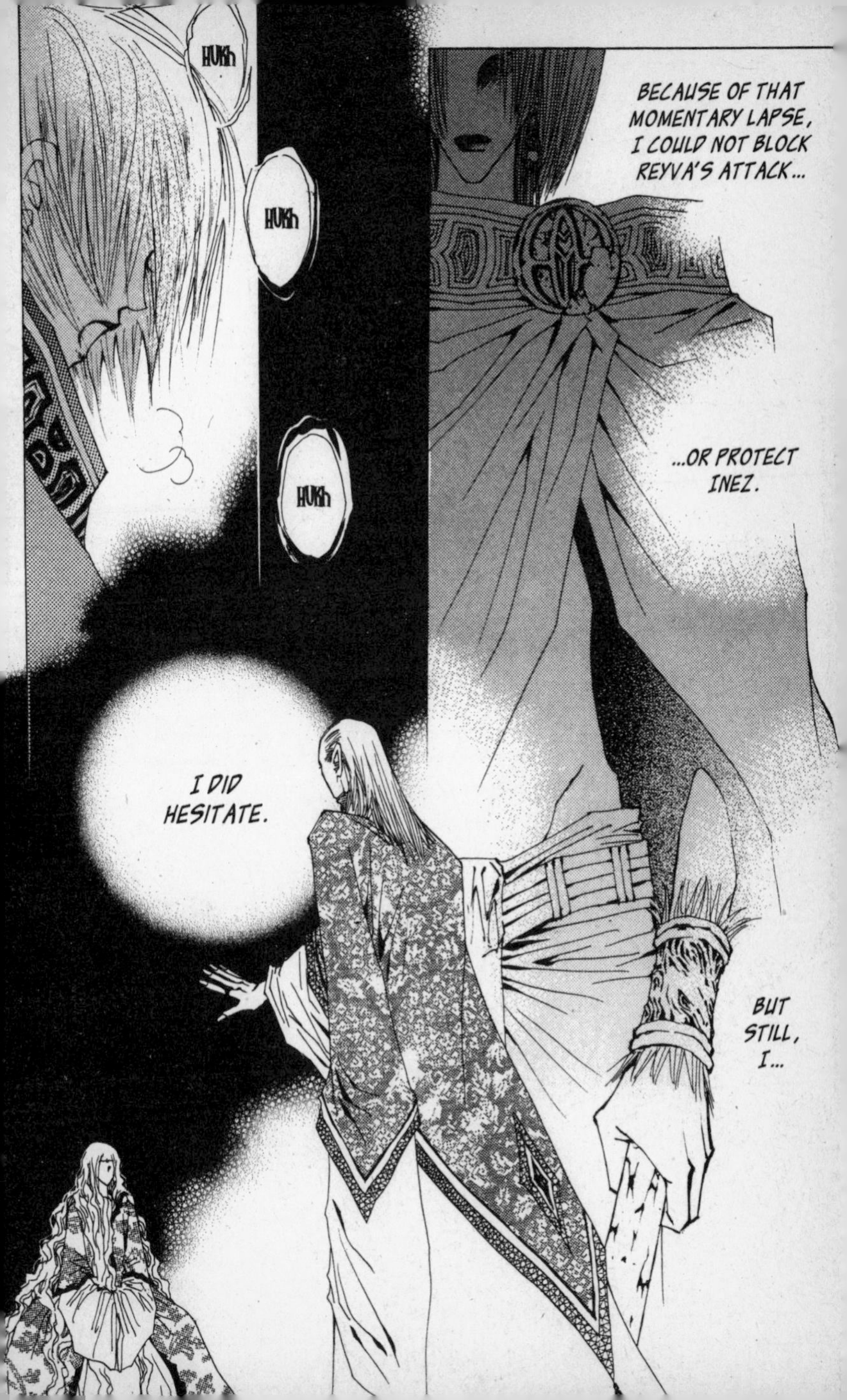
HUKh
HUKh
HUKh
BECAUSE OF THAT MOMENTARY LAPSE, I COULD NOT BLOCK REYVA'S ATTACK...
...OR PROTECT INEZ.
I DID HESITATE.
BUT STILL, I...

THIS IS DANGEROUS...
OUR JOURNEY MIGHT END...
...IN DISASTER!
...HESITATED!

HEY! FINALLY AWAKE?
NOW THAT I'VE HAD A CHANCE TO LOOK AROUND THIS PLACE, IT'S NOT HALF BAD. THANKS TO YOU, SLEEPYHEAD, I HAVE A WHOLE NEW APPRECIATION FOR EAST GARDEN.
HEY, WHY ARE YOU LOOKING AT ME LIKE THAT? I'M FINE, EXCEPT FOR SOME SORE MUSCLES. THE HALF-ELF NURSED ME.
NOW DON'T GET ALL MUSHY ON ME AND THANK ME FOR SAVING YOUR LIFE.

KYRETTE...
NICE WEATHER, DON'T YOU THINK?
AH...
I WANT TO ASK WHY YOU PROTECTED ME WHEN IT COULD HAVE GOTTEN YOU KILLED. WHY DID YOU...

I DON'T KNOW WHO YOU ARE.
OR WHY YOU'RE BEING SO KIND TO ME.
BUT...
I WANT TO THANK YOU...FROM THE BOTTOM OF MY HEART.
I REALIZE THAT NOTHING ELSE MATTERS...
...WHEN LIFE IS AT STAKE.

WE CAN'T GUARANTEE REANA'S RECOVERY NOW THAT THE SPELL-CASTER HAS DIED WITHOUT UNDOING THE SPELL.
EVEN IF SHE NEVER WAKES UP AGAIN...
...THANK YOU FOR ALLOWING ME TO STAY BY HER SIDE LIKE THIS.
I'LL NEVER GIVE UP.
I KNOW I'LL HEAR REANA'S VOICE AGAIN SOMEDAY.
WHEN THAT DAY COMES...I'LL HAVE SOMETHING TO TELL HER.

I'LL TELL HER THAT I'VE KEPT MY PROMISE...
DON'T GIVE UP ON ME, ARIEL....
...THAT I'LL STAY BY HER SIDE FOREVER TO KEEP THAT PROMISE...
THEY LOOKED HAPPY TOGETHER.
REANA WAS ASLEEP, BUT I COULD FEEL HAPPINESS ON HER FACE.

ARE LOVERS HAPPY JUST TO BE WITH EACH OTHER...
...EVEN IF THEY CAN'T SEE THE SAME SKY?
DON'T YOU REMEMBER BLATHERING ABOUT LOVE WHEN YOU RAN INTO YULAN'S ARMS?
BUT DIDN'T YOU SAY THAT TRUE LOVE NEVER HURTS?
WHAT ARE YOU TALKING ABOUT?

YULAN'S... ARMS?
DON'T BE RIDICULOUS! I DIDN'T RUN INTO ANYTHING!!
WHY ARE YOU BLUSHING? AREN'T YOU TWO INVOLVED?
IN...VOLVED?
DON'T YOU LIKE HIM, AND DOESN'T HE LIKE YOU?
Ping
WASN'T THIS WHOLE TRIP A LOVERS' ESCAPE IN THE FIRST PLACE?
THE WAY YOU LOOKED AT EACH OTHER ALMOST MADE ME BARF!

HEY KID, I'M TALKING TO YOU!
THIS MAN IS BEYOND SAVING!
휭
grin
THE POWER OF ELVES IS AMAZING...
THEY SAY HALF-ELVES ARE SOMETIMES GIFTED WITH EVEN GREATER HEALING POWERS THAN PUREBLOODED ELVES...
...BUT I NEVER KNEW THAT I WOULD EXPERIENCE IT PERSONALLY...

ARIEL HAS AN AMAZING ABILITY TO FIGHT INFECTION, AND HIS POWERS CAN EVEN BE TRANSMITTED TO OTHERS.
TO BE ABLE TO HEAL...
IF ONLY HUMANS COULD COMMAND SUCH POWERS...
YOU HAVE TO KEEP YOUR PROMISE...
RACHEL...
GRUNCH

WHAT? YOU HAVE SOMETHING LEFT TO SAY--
?!

HMPFH. NO FEELING WHATSOEVER!
JUST LIKE LAST TIME.
I DON'T KNOW WHY PEOPLE ENJOY THIS SO MUCH. I ASKED GRANDPA ONCE, AND HE SAID THAT I'LL JUST NATURALLY COME TO UNDERSTAND IT ONE DAY.

I'VE ALWAYS BEEN CURIOUS TO KNOW WHAT A KISS FELT LIKE. HAVING THE ELF-LORD KISS ME WHEN I WAS PRETENDING TO BE REANA WAS MY FIRST KISS EVER.
ALL I COULD FEEL WAS FEAR. AND HOW COLD HIS LIPS WERE.
I THOUGHT IT MIGHT BE DIFFERENT WITH YOU, BUT NO, NOTHING. ZILCH!
WHAT'S SO EXCITING ABOUT PRESSING LIPS TOGETHER?
DID I PRESS TOO HARD? MY LIPS HURT.
SORRY, I CAME BACK BECAUSE I GOT CURIOUS ALL OF A SUDDEN.
WHEN I GET CURIOUS, I CAN'T WAIT.
STOP RIGHT THERE!

DON'T YOU UNDERSTAND WHAT YOU JUST DID?
YOU HURT MY PRIDE!

WE WILL LEAVE EARLY TOMORROW MORNING. WE'VE WASTED TOO MUCH TIME HERE.
O-OKAY.
WHAT DO I DO? I CAN'T LOOK HIM IN THE EYE...!

AS YOU COMMANDED, I GAVE YULAN THE THING YOU GAVE ME.
WELL DONE.
...SO YULAN HAS GONE.
YES, MY LORD. AND HIS COMPANIONS TOO.
I'M HAPPY THAT I WAS ABLE TO GIVE IT TO HIM BEFORE MY LIFE IS OVER.
WHEN WILL HIS WANDERINGS END, I WONDER...?

CLOP
CLOP
...THANK YOU.

I WAS ABLE TO PROTECT REANA, THANKS TO YOU.
I THANK YOU FOR YOUR COURAGE AND GREAT KINDNESS ONCE AGAIN.
SUCH WARMTH...
BUT...
HIS TOUCH IS SO WARM AND COMFORTING. IT REMINDS ME OF GRANDFATHER...

...THAT OTHER KISS WAS DIFFERENT. I PRETENDED NOT TO NOTICE BECAUSE IT WAS SUCH A SURPRISE...
DIFFERENT FROM THE ELF-LORD'S, AND DIFFERENT FROM ARIEL'S.
...BUT KYRETTE'S KISS WAS DIFFERENT!

IT SENT CHILLS DOWN MY SPINE!
WHY? WHY WAS IT DIFFERENT?
I WISH I'D NEVER KISSED HIM!

BOW
AND NOW I CAN'T EVEN LOOK YULAN IN THE FACE!
THINKING ABOUT IT STILL MAKES ME BLUSH.
화끈
YULAN, I DON'T SEE KYRETTE. WHAT HAPPENED TO HIM?
WHERE'S KYRETTE?
WAIT A MINUTE...

YOU HAVE THE HEARTSBLOOD PENDANT WITH YOU, RIGHT?
OF COURSE! WHY ARE YOU ASKING *NOW?*
JUST CHECKIN TO SEE THAT YOU HAVEN'T FORGOTTEN TH PURPOSE OF THIS MISSION.
I TOLD YOU BEFORE AND I'M SAYING IT AGAIN NOW. YOUR UNNECESSARY CURIOSITY WILL ONLY GET YOU INTO TROUBLE. DIDN'T THIS INCIDENT TEACH YOU ANYTHING?
YOUR STUBBORNNES PUT OTHERS I DANGER.

I WON'T LET YOU JEOPARDIZE OUR MISSION FOR SUCH TRIVIALITIES AGAIN.
WHAT? TRIVIALITIES?
HOW...CAN YOU SAY THAT? LIVES WERE AT STAKE.
WAS REANA'S TRAGEDY JUST A TRIVIALITY TO YOU?

YES, IT WAS DANGEROUS, BUT TO ME, IT'S MORE IMPORTANT TO HELP THOSE IN NEED...
...THAN TO GO LOOK FOR SOME DRAGON!
I'M REALLY DISAPPOINTED! I DIDN'T KNOW YOU THOUGHT THAT WAY.
I THOUGHT YOU HAD A TENDER HEART UNDERNEATH THAT TOUGH SHELL.
THAT YOU DID WHAT YOU DID BECAUSE YOU FELT COMPASSION...
AND NOW YOU SAY THAT IT WAS ALL USELESS CURIOSITY. A MERE TRIVIALITY!

JUST COME RIGHT OUT AND SAY IT!
YOU CONSIDER ME UNFIT TO CARRY OUT THIS GREAT MISSION!
THE FACT THAT I'M A GIRL MAKES YOU NERVOUS!

GOOD. AS LONG AS I GO WITH THEM, IT'S BETTER IF YOU STAY AWAY.
WE CAN'T LET YULAN REALIZE WHO YOU ARE.
BUT THERE'S ONE THING THAT I CAN'T UNDERSTAND.
SOMEONE BLOCKED MY SWORD FROM BEING SUMMONED.
...I'LL SEND ALONG ANOTHER TO ASSIST YOU IN MY PLACE FROM NOW ON.

I'M SURE IT WAS AN ELF.
HIS POWER WAS THAT OF A HIGH ELF.
BUT NOT EVERY HIGH ELF CAN BLOCK MY SWORD.
IN OTHER WORDS... THIS ELF WAS SOMEHOW CONNECTED TO MY SWORD.
DO YOU HAVE ANY IDEA WHO IT MIGHT BE?

EVEN WE CAN'T DETERMINE THE EXACT AGE OF THAT SWORD.
ALL WE KNOW IS THAT IT HAS CHANGED HANDS MANY, MANY TIMES OVER THE CENTURIES.
DOES THIS MEAN THAT ONE OF THE SWORD'S PREVIOUS OWNERS MIGHT STILL BE ALIVE?
Chirp
Chirp

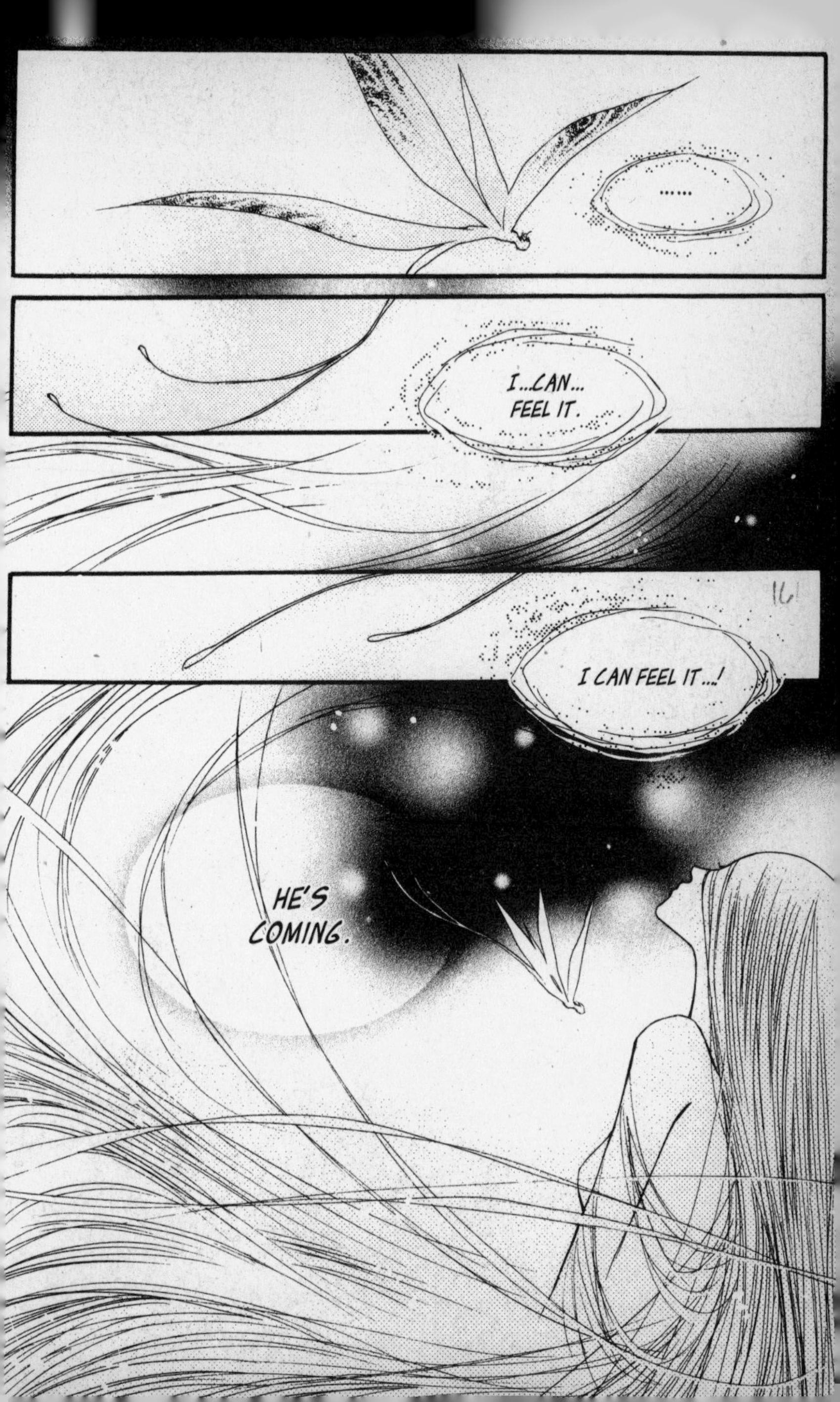
......
I...CAN... FEEL IT.
I CAN FEEL IT...!
HE'S COMING.

MONG!
I'M SORRY, MONG, BUT I WANT TO BE ALONE RIGHT NOW. ASK YULAN TO PLAY WITH YOU.
MONG.
MONG.
MONG.
MONG.
SHE'S COMING...

WHAT'S GOING ON? MY BODY SUDDENLY FEELS HEAVY AS ROCKS.
THE KID'S HORSE IS HERE, WHICH MUST MEAN THAT SHE'S AROUND HERE SOMEWHERE, TOO...
Whak
!
INEZ...?

Episode 5:
Dream Parasite

OUCH!
MY HEAD FEELS LIKE IT'S GOING T
EXPLODE...
YULAN-
YULAN!

SHOW YOURSELVES RIGHT NOW!!
GOD, EVERY TIME I LOSE CONSCIOUSNESS, I WAKE UP IN A DIFFERENT PLACE ALTOGETHER!
YULAN! KYRETTE!
WHERE IS VERYONE?!
WHERE ARE YOU BOTH? YUL...
WHOA!

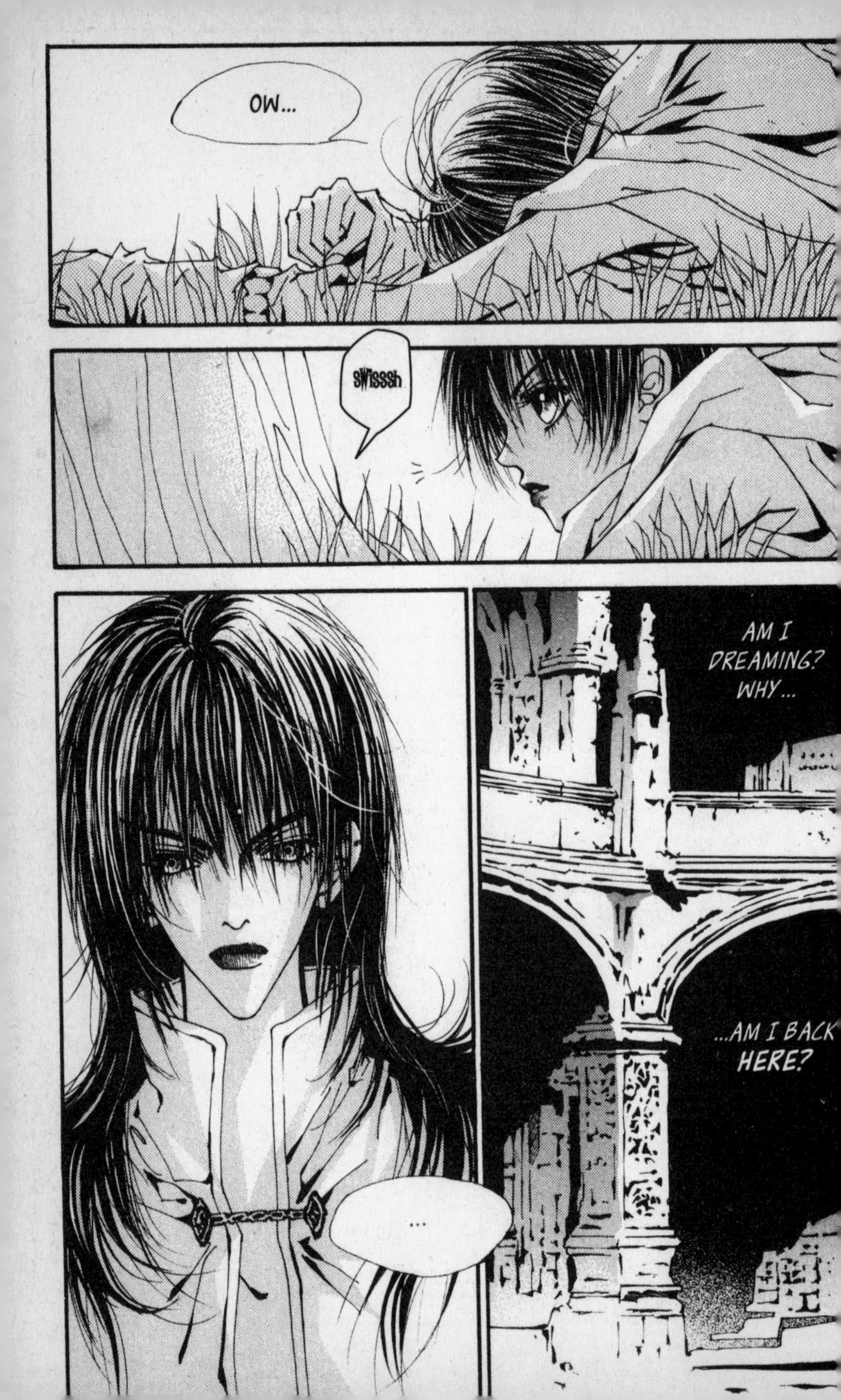
OW...
SWISSSH
AM I DREAMING? WHY...
...AM I BACK HERE?
...

THIS WAY.
WHAT... WHAT KIND OF SICK JOKE IS THIS?

WE MUST MOURN YOUR FATHER'S DEATH, KYRETTE. HE LIES IN ETERNAL REST NOW.
HE'S NOT MY FATHER.
MY FATHER DIED A LONG TIME AGO.
HE WAS KILLED BY THE MAN LYING THERE.

KYRETTE!
KYRETTE!
SO I DON'T HAVE ANY TEARS TO SHED FOR HIM.

MONG!
MOST DEFINITELY A DREAM!
BECAUSE IF IT WASN'T A DREAM, I WOULDN'T BE WEARING THIS--
--THIS RIDICULOUSLY REVEALING GOWN!
IT'S COMPLETELY SEE-THROUGH!
THIS IS ONLY A DREAM!

YOU'RE SO BEAUTIFUL.
THOUGH YOU ARE NOT YET MATURE ENOUGH TO COMMAND A VOLUPTUOUS SILHOUETTE.
...MY DEVOTION TO YOU WILL NEVER CHANGE, NO MATTER HOW DIFFERENT YOU LOOK.
I NEVER EXPECTED YOU TO APPEAR IN THIS FORM.
WHAT?
HOWEVER...

I WON'T LET ZEYER TAKE YOU FROM ME, NOT THIS TIME.
I'M THE ONE WHO HAS DISCOVERED YOU NOW.
WHAT IS SHE TALKING ABOUT? I DON'T UNDERSTAND A THING SHE'S SAYING.
WHO IS SHE? AND WHO'S ZEYER? IS SHE CRAZY?

I WOULD LIKE TO ASK YOU ONE SMALL THING.
MAY I HAVE YOUR PERMISSION TO KILL ZEYER?

WHAT'S HAPPENED?
I DON'T KNOW WHY. I CAME OVER HERE AND ALL OF A SUDDEN, MY BODY WENT ALL HEAVY.
AS YOU SEE, THE KID'S STILL ASLEEP.
I LOST CONSCIOUSNESS FOR A WHILE TOO, I THINK.
I THINK I HAD SOME KIND OF DREAM, BUT I CAN'T REMEMBER A THING.
ALL I HAVE LEFT IS A SPLITTING HEADACHE.

LILITH... COULD IT BE LILITH AGAIN?
YOU SAID YOU HAD A DREAM.
CONCENTRATE. TRY TO REMEMBER WHAT IT WAS ABOUT.

WHAT? ARE YOU TRYING TO SAY THAT MY DREAM IS CONNECTED TO OUR REALITY?
I'LL ASK JUST ONCE MORE. MAY I KILL ZEYER?
YOU HAVE TO REMEMBER YOUR DREAM. THAT'S THE ONLY WAY YOU CAN GET OUT FROM UNDER HER HYPNOTIC SPELL.

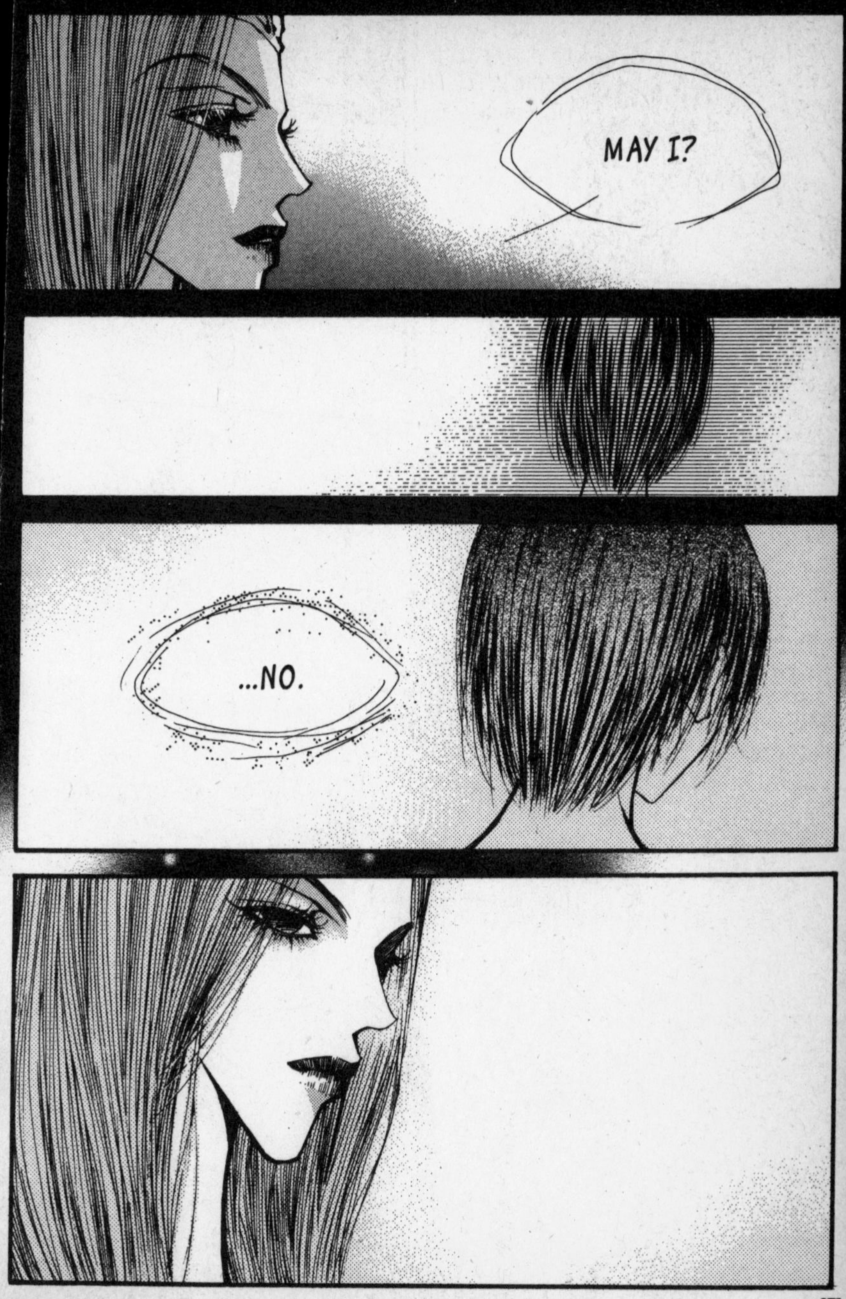
MAY I?
...NO.

SO, YOU HAVEN'T CHANGED.
THE SHELL HAS CHANGED, BUT NOT YOU.
I'LL REMEMBER YOUR COMMAND. BUT I CAN'T ALWAYS CONTROL MY MOODS.
...YOU ARE NOT PERMITTED TO TOUCH EVEN A SINGLE HAIR ON HER HEAD.
ZEYER IS MINE.
REMEMBER THAT.

I CAN'T HELP FEELING JEALOUS OF THOSE WHOM YOU CHERISH.
SEND ME BACK.
NOT BEFORE YOU TELL ME ONE THING.
IS IT BECAUSE OF ZEYER?
I MEAN THE REASON YOU CHOSE THAT PARTICULAR PHYSICAL FORM...?

ABABA BABA.
CHOMP
CHOMP
UBABA ABA--
UBABA...
HEY, SPEAK HUMAN, WILL YOU? WHAT'S THE MATTER?
ABA...

I'M SO HUNGRY.
I DON'T KNOW WHY...BUT I'M STARVING.
HRRUCK
I KNEW SOMETHING LIKE THIS WOULD HAPPEN. YOU MADE YOURSELF SICK WITH ALL THAT EATING.
LET IT ALL OUT, COME ON.
탁탁
GAG
GAG

EXCEPT FOR HUNGER, I CAN'T REMEMBER A SINGLE THING.
I CAN'T EVEN BELIEVE THAT I WAS OUT THAT LONG.
DID YOU FALL ASLEEP TOO, KYRETTE?
YULAN, DO YOU MEAN THAT THERE'S SOME MESSAGE HIDDEN INSIDE OUR DREAMS?
YEAH, I HAD DREAMS TOO. BUT I CAN'T REMEMBER ANYTHING EITHER.
I'M NOT ABSOLUTELY CERTAIN, BUT IF THE PERSON BEHIND ALL THIS IS WHO I THINK SHE IS, WE HAVE TO KEEP OUR GUARD UP.
GUARD UP?
YULAN SAYS WE HAVE TO REMEMBER OUR DREAMS IF WE WANT TO ESCAPE THEIR HYPNOTIC CONTROL.

ONE OF YOU MAY BECOME HER PUPPET.
SHE IS THE ONE WHO DISTURBS REST.
PUP...PET?
THAT'S RIDICULOUS. YOU FALL ASLEEP FOR A LITTLE WHILE, AND ALL OF A SUDDEN YOU'VE FALLEN UNDER SOME EVIL WITCH'S CONTROL?
WHO IS SHE, ANYWAY?

...HER NAME IS LILITH.
A PARASITE THAT DWELLS WITHIN THE DREAMS OF ALL THAT LIVE.

...STOP PRETENDING TO BE ASLEEP.
HOW ABOUT A LITTLE WAGER?
WHO WILL HE... I MEAN SHE, NOW...

...CHOOSE?
YOU, MY LOVELY ZEYER?
OR...

YULAN, WHAT'S WRONG? DO YOU SEE SOMETHING?
AH.
NO.
YOU SCARED ME, STOPPING LIKE THAT ALL OF A SUDDEN.

DON'T WORRY, ZEYER. I'M ON YOUR SIDE.
I WON'T LET MY LOVELY LITTLE BROTHER GET HURT.
AND I CAN'T LET HIM BE DEFEATED NOW, CAN I...?

TO BE CONTINUED IN ARCANA VOLUME 4!

THE QUEST CONTINUES IN

ARCANA

VOLUME 4

HIDDEN AGENDAS AND LONG DORMANT PERSONALITIES COME TO THE SURFACE. WE LEARN MORE ABOUT THE TRUE NATURE OF INEZ'S SPECIAL GIFT. YULAN AND INEZ'S RELATIONSHIP IS PUT TO THE TEST WHEN IT BECOMES CLEAR THAT HIS FEELINGS FOR HER GO DEEPER THAN ANYONE COULD HAVE GUESSED. AND AS WE UNCOVER MORE ABOUT THE MOTIVATIONS OF THE SECRETIVE KYRETTE, IT APPEARS THAT HIS INTENTIONS, WHILE NOBLE, MAY STILL PROVE DISASTROUS FOR THE KINGDOM INEZ HAS SWORN TO PROTECT. THERE'S INTRIGUE AND ADVENTURE IN EVERY PAGE OF THE NEXT VOLUME OF ARCANA!

BY SANG-SUN PARK

By the creator of ARK ANGELS

THE TAROT CAFÉ

I was always kind of fond of *Petshop of Horrors,* and then along comes *The Tarot Café* and blows me away. It's like *Petshop,* but with a bishonen factor that goes through the roof and into the stratosphere! Sang-Sun Park's art is just unreal. It's beautifully detailed, all the characters are stunning and unique, and while at first the story seems to be yet another Gothy episodic piece of fluff, there is a dark side to Pamela and her powers that I can't wait to read more about. I'm a sucker for teenage werewolves, too.

~Lillian Diaz-Pryzbyl, Editor

BY SVETLANA CHMAKOVA

DRAMACON

I love this manga! First of all, Svetlana is amazing. She's the artist who creates "The Adventures of CosmoGIRL!" manga feature in *CosmoGIRL!* magazine, and she totally rules. *Dramacon* is a juicy romance about a guy and a girl who meet up every year at a crazy anime convention. It grabbed me from the first panel and just wouldn't let go. If you love shojo as much as I do, this book will rock your world.

~Julie Taylor, Senior Editor

Ark Angels
TOKYOPOP
Sang-Sun Park